STAND FIRM TO THE END

PREPARING FOR THE END OF DAYS

FORREST GARVIN

ACKNOWLEDGMENTS

I would like to give a shout out to:

Mark Gott, Kyle Plessinger,

Tenderfoot, and Tom Young for their help

and constant encouragement.

TABLE OF CONTENTS

PREPARING FOR THE
END OF DAYS

You will hear of wars and rumors of wars, but see to it that you are not alarmed. Such things must happen, but the end is still to come.7 Nation will rise against nation, and kingdom against kingdom. There will be famines and earthquakes in various places.8 All these are the beginning of birth pains.
Matthew 24:6-8

Ever since Jesus Christ walked the face of the Earth, people have speculated about the end of days. We know they are coming because He told us so. A considerable amount of scripture deals with the End Times, over and above the entire Book of Revelations. But one thing that the Bible doesn't give us is a date on the calendar, so that we know when it will come.

As we have suffered our way through 2020 and its many crises, there have been those who have said that the end is near. They may be right; but then again, all the others who have said that the end was near in the past, during other difficult years, were wrong. So what makes those who are saying that COVID-19 is a sign of the end so sure they are any more right than all the people who were wrong before?

We need to remember that there have been those who were talking about the return of the risen Lord in the Early Church. Paul deals with this subject briefly in both 1 Corinthians and 2 Thessalonians. So this is clearly not a new area of speculation, nor is it new that believers believe the signs of the times are indicating that the end is nigh.

The reality is that we don't know when the end will come. God did that deliberately so we would have to live by faith. If the Lord had given us a date for His return, there are those who would have lived for the devil until the day before and then confessed the Lord as their Savior.

We just don't know. We must continue living our lives here on Earth as if we will live out our days. Yet at the same time, we must be ready to go at any moment. As someone once put, "We must live with our suitcase in one hand, ready to go, and our hammer in the other, working until that day comes." I am quite sure that God would have us do no less.

But just what does this mean? What can we expect? Where does this journey called life lead us between now and the time of the Lord's return? What do we need to do and how can we be ready for it?

Matthew 24, verses 6 though 8, written above, make it clear that we can expect problems… lots of them. Have there been wars and rumors of wars? Yes, there have. Has nation risen against nation? They've never stopped. What about famines and earthquakes? Both exist in abundance. In fact, all of these things have existed since the time of Jesus, and it doesn't look like any of them are about to call it quits any time soon.

There have been many who have looked to this laundry list as if it were a checklist of items that would occur before the Lord's return. But the Lord never said it was: he just warned us what was to come. Yes, He says, "And then the end will come," but if we look at it more carefully, we see that's directly connected to the gospel being preached in all the world:

"And this gospel of the kingdom shall be preached in all the world for a witness unto all nations; and then the end will come" (Matthew 24:14).

Can these words be taken to refer to the previous verses? Yes they can. Many have. But that doesn't mean it has to be. Nor does it mean that we are correct in doing so. All we can say for sure is that those things will happen before the end comes, not that they are a sign of the end coming.

I realize I'm being a bit picky here, but there is a reason for that. We all tend to have our own ideas about what scripture means - mostly things we've been taught. But that sometimes means that we are accepting as truth things that scripture doesn't actually say. There's a real danger in that, and it's something we really should work hard to avoid.

Let me give you a simple example of what I mean. In Genesis, chapter 18, three angels appeared to Abraham. Either recognizing who they were or just being a good host, he arranged for a meal to be prepared for them. Once they had eaten, they asked:

"Where is your wife Sarah?" "There in the tent," he said.[10] Then the Lord said, "I will surely return to you about this time next year, and Sarah your wife will have a son..."[11] Abraham and Sarah were already old and well advanced in years, and Sarah was past the age of childbearing.[12] So Sarah laughed to herself as she thought, "After I am worn out and my master is old, will I now have this pleasure?" (Genesis 18:9-12).

You've probably heard a description of Sarah based on these verses, that she was old, decrepit, and wrinkled. I sure have - many times. But that is not necessarily true. Two chapters later, Abraham says that Sarah is his sister, and she ends up in King Abimelech's harem (Genesis 20:2), even though she was ninety years old.

Now, in case you didn't know it, kings can be rather picky about the women that end up in their harems. So, while I wasn't there, I'm pretty sure that Abimelech wasn't looking for old, wrinkled women to join his harem. He wanted beautiful women, just like any other man would. So even though Sarah was old, by our reckoning, she clearly didn't look it. She was beautiful.

By the way, we see in scripture that Sarah does give birth to a baby one year later. He was named Isaac.

So why do I say all this? I'm merely trying to dissuade you from trying to use Matthew chapter 24 as a checklist for the End Times. Besides, that checklist doesn't seem to say anything about a worldwide pandemic, so it doesn't really fit 2020, no matter how hard we try.

Nevertheless, events like the COVID-19 pandemic remind us of how fragile life is and that we are headed into a time when we can expect an increase in disasters around the world. Jesus referred to this time as the "beginning of birth pains" in verse 8 above and as the "beginning of sorrows" in the King James Version.

So just what is this time that Jesus is referring to? It is a time before the events foretold in the Book of Revelations, when things get worse here in the world. It is a time when the effects of sin are at their worst, causing huge imbalances in nature and resulting in catastrophic disasters.

You may be wondering how I can say that things will get worse here in the world. It comes from the truth taught to us in Romans 6:23 *"the wages of sin is death."* That being true, we can easily see that there was no death before sin. In other words, there was no death before the fall in Genesis chapter 3. Many theologians and preachers have taken this to mean that the very first death in the world were the animals God killed to make clothing for Adam and Eve, in Genesis 3:21.

We also find where it says that there will be an increase of wickedness, or sin, in the same chapter of Matthew's gospel, specifically in verse 12. Since sin always has consequences, an increase in sin should lead to an increase in consequences.

That's what we're facing today - an increase in consequences. Since sin isn't coming to an end, and will in fact continue to increase, it only makes sense to expect more consequences. Hence, we enter into the time Jesus refers to as the "beginning of sorrows" or the "beginning of birth pains."

This naturally raises the question of whether or not we are already in that time, a question that's hard to answer. But if we go back to the original verses, there in Matthew chapter 24, we find that we are. We are already experiencing many of the things that Jesus refers to as the beginning of sorrows.

For that matter, it is reasonable to say that we have been in the beginning of sorrows since the time of Jesus, since the disasters that Jesus talks about in those verses have been happening since then. Were we to track them through history, we would find that they have waxed and waned but they have happened. Right now, we're in a time when they seem to be increasing.

We need to be careful about this, though. It is easy to think that the disasters we are facing today are worse than those that have been faced in the past. But that's a very hard comparison to make accurately. There is no universal scale of disasters, where we can award each disaster a point value and add up the total points for a year. Even if we tried to come up with such a scale, it would be flawed, as any disaster can vary in scope and size, as well as in intensity and overall impact.

What we can be sure of is that disasters are here to stay. Not only have we seen a number of other disasters occur during the time of COVID-19, but we have had to deal with multiple disasters at once. When Hurricane Hanna (2008) came to call, we were also dealing with rioting in many cities and still dealing with shortages caused by the pandemic. From the way things look right now, it seems that multiple disasters at once may be becoming the norm.

Part of what makes this so is that COVID-19 is not going to disappear as many hope. Ever since the pandemic started, there have been those who have been talking about a vaccine; but while there is much work going on to develop such a vaccine, it is becoming less and less likely that one will actually work – and soon.

To start with, the first problem in developing a vaccine is that the process is rather prolonged. The shortest time that a vaccine has ever been developed and approved is four years. Yet somehow people think that our medical community can develop a vaccine for a totally new virus in just a few months. Well, it's been a few months, and it hasn't happened yet. Even Dr. Faucci is saying that he is doubtful that a successful vaccine will be developed, and he's defining a "successful vaccine" as one that works 50% of the time.

The next issue is that antibodies from having COVID-19 only last a few weeks in the body, maybe as long as two months; that's it. But the purpose of a vaccine is to cause the body's autoimmune system to produce antibodies that will attack the virus. So even if they do develop a vaccine that works, it will only produce a result that lasts a couple of months at the most. What are we going to do? Vaccinate the whole world every two months to destroy the virus?

Then there's the issue of those who won't take the vaccine anyway. Taking any new medicine is risky, even more so for a vaccine. Even though the vaccine is tested on a large number of people in phase three clinical trials, there's still some risk. Being one of the first to take the vaccine puts any of us in the position of accepting that risk.

With the large number of people in our country who have developed an "anti-vaccine" attitude, as well as those who think the whole thing is a conspiracy cooked up to take our rights away, chances are there won't be enough people willing to take any disease they come up with to destroy the virus.

All this leads us to the conclusion that COVID-19 is going to be around for years to come. It would have to mutate to a point where it was so deadly that everyone became scared of it. Before We the People would accept mandatory vaccination. I don't think that's going to happen.

So, whatever disaster happens in the future, even several years in the future, will happen in a world with

COVID-19. You and I are going to have to face multiple disasters at once, dealing with the current disease, and any future diseases and disasters, all as one integrated disaster. It will be challenging, but we're going to have to figure out how to do it.

Definitely sounds like sorrows to me.

A Closer Look at Matthew 24

As we've already defined, we're living in a time that Jesus referred to as the beginning of sorrows. That's a rather appropriate name, considering the sorrow that tends to accompany any disaster. The other name for this time, the beginning of birth pains, is just as appropriate, as the pain of these various disasters will be with us until the time of the Great Tribulation begins.

Even though Matthew 24 isn't a checklist of things that will usher in the End Times, it is a list of things we can expect to have to deal with. These things have already been happening, and there's no reason to think that they will stop any time soon.

You and I must learn how to live with the things

occurring around us. A large part of it is trusting in God as our protector. Our faith in Him is critical to not only our survival, but also to our dependence on His protection and provision through trying times.

In Hebrews, chapter 11, the great "Hall of Faith," we see examples of how many biblical characters used their faith to obey God and do what He told them to do. In some of those cases, they were going into dangerous situations, needing to trust God to take care of them in the midst of that danger. Noah built the ark and escaped the flood because of his faith. Had his faith faltered, he might have died along with everyone else. Abraham left his home and crossed a desert to inherit a new land because of his faith. Had he missed God, he could have gone to the wrong place and perished in the desert. Moses' parents hid him for three months, knowing that if he was found, it was a death sentence for them.

God doesn't expect us to be perfect, but He does expect us to have faith. As it says in the next chapter, just after the Hall of Faith:

"Let us throw off everything that hinders and the sin that so easily entangles, and let us run with perseverance the race marked out for us.[2] Let us fix our eyes on Jesus, the author and perfecter of our faith" (Hebrews 12:1-2).

This is not the kind of faith that tries to use God as some celestial vending machine that passes out blessings. That's not what Hebrews 11 is about. Those heroes used their faith to obey God. Through that obedience, they received the promises that He had given them. That's a bit different than deciding that we want God to give us something and then using our faith to try and get it. While I won't say that God won't ever give someone something they ask Him for, He is much more likely to give them what He promises them. The two are clearly not the same thing.

We will need God's protection in the times to come. But we will also need to do our part. Our obedience, coupled with our faith, will open the door for God's provision, God's protection, and God's guidance through these difficult times. That will get us through the beginning of sorrows.

Keep in mind that the beginning of sorrows comes before any of the events of the Tribulation. This means that none of us will get out of the difficulties and hardships of that time unless we die. However, through the proper use of our faith and obedience to God, we can be protected during those times. That doesn't mean that we won't see any hardship ourselves; it does mean that we won't have to face that hardship alone. We will have God at our sides, leading us through it, with His grace filling in to help us out, wherever we fall short.

It doesn't matter what End Times theology we subscribe to; some believe that the rapture will happen before the Tribulation, while others believe it will happen afterwards. But we're not talking about the Tribulation here; we're talking about events and trials that will come before. The wars, famines, persecution, and other things that Jesus talked about will come before any of that begins. So, even if you believe in a pre-tribulation rapture, like most believers do, don't think that will get you out of the beginning of sorrows. It won't.

Jesus gave his disciples the admonition about the coming of wars and other disasters in direct response to them asking Him how to tell that the end is coming.

As Jesus was sitting on the Mount of Olives, the disciples came to him privately, "Tell us," they said, "when will this happen, and what will be the sign of your coming and of the end of the age." (Matthew 24:3).

What's interesting is that Jesus starts His response by saying, "Watch out that no one deceives you" (Matthew 24:4). Obviously, He knew that some would try to do just that. Then he gives some specific types of deception that His disciples should be careful of.

"For many will come in my name, claiming, 'I am the Christ, and will deceive many.[6] You will hear of wars and rumors of wars, but see to it that you are not alarmed. Such things must happen, but the end is still to come.[7] Nation will rise against nation, and kingdom against kingdom. There will be famines and earthquakes in various places.[8] All these are the beginning of birth pains." (Matthew 24:5-8).

Notice the underlined part. It tells us three distinct, but interrelated, things. First, we are not to be alarmed. If anything is going to get us through what is to come, it is our faith in God. Not necessarily the faith that we confess with our mouths, but the faith that we have in our hearts. Faith starts there; and if it isn't there, then the confession coming out of our mouths really isn't faith.

Why shouldn't we be alarmed? Because regardless of how things look, God has it all under control. That's the second thing we see, where it says that the wars and other disasters must happen. While those things may not be God's best; he knows about them. He has already planned for them. They have to happen. Why? Because each and every one of them are necessary in order for God's ultimate plan for the End Days to be fulfilled. That should be comforting to us.

The third thing Jesus said there is that those things will be happening before the end comes. In other words, they will happen before the events written about in the Book of Revelations.

There's almost a hint here that things are going to get worse than the wars and disasters he is talking about. If we look at the verses that follow, we can see that is the case, at least if we look at it from a personal basis. I don't think any of us like the idea of being turned over to be persecuted.

But it's the line after that which is important to us.

"But he who stands to the end will be saved." (Matthew 24:13).

This has to be our goal. We must become those who are

ready to stand until the end. That can be taken in a spiritual context; but it can also be taken in a physical one. If we are going to fulfill what we are called to do, we must do both.

So just what does it mean to "stand?" Spiritually, it means keeping the faith, without wavering. We must remember who we are in Christ and who He is in us. We must not allow the world to turn us away from Him. And we must continue to trust in Him, no matter what problems come our way.

Physically, standing means being ready to walk through those problems, regardless of what form they take. While we can expect God's help, we can't just sit on our backsides and expect him to do it all. There are too many believers today who are saying, "God will have to do it" about things that God is specifically telling them to do.

Is God telling us to stand? Yes He is. There are a number of verses in the Bible that talk about how we should be ready to deal with problems and how we should stand up to them.

"Those who work their land will have abundant food but those who chase fantasies will have their fill of poverty" (Proverbs 28:19).

"The wise store up choice food and olive oil, but fools gulp theirs down" (Proverbs 21:20).

"Anyone who does not provide for their relative, and especially for those of their own household, has denied the faith and is worse than an unbeliever" (1 Timothy 5:8).

"The prudent see danger and take refuge, but the simple keep going and pay the penalty" (Proverbs 22:3).

"He said to them, "But now if you have a purse, take it, and also a bag; and if you don't have a sword, sell your cloak and buy one" (Luke 22:36).

There are more, but we'll leave it at this. The point I want you to see is that our physical preparation is important too, not just our spiritual preparation. Yes, by all means, prepare yourself spiritually to stand. But don't stop there; learn how to stand on your own two feet and not just depend on the government to take care of you. God never intended for the government to do that.

There's one other area in this chapter I want to look at - what we are instructed to do, when a disaster comes.

"Then let those who are in Judah flee to the mountains.[17] Let no one on the roof of his house go down to take anything out of the house [18] Let no one in the field go back to get his cloak" (Mathew 24:16-18).

Let's put this in context. This isn't talking about wars and rumors of wars. It's not talking about famine and earthquakes. It's not even talking about persecution. It is a specific reference to a particular event, referred to as "the abomination that causes desolation" (Matthew 24:15).

While many different events could be referred to by this title, theologians agree that it specifically refers to the Roman Army besieging Jerusalem. They were the abomination, causing desolation by desecrating the temple.

That may seem a bit odd, since Judah was under Roman control at the time. But the Roman Army destroyed Jerusalem and the Temple in 70AD. That's what it refers to.

Can it have a secondary meaning? Yes it can. Prophecy often has a double reference, referring to two separate events, which are thousands of years apart. The only problem is that it is more or less impossible to tell what events it refers to until after the fact. We'll have to wait and see.

Nevertheless, when we combine those verses with the ones listed earlier, we can see that there's a possibility of them going together. The wars and rumors of wars referred to can very well be associated with a new abomination that will cause desolation. So we shouldn't ignore the possibility of that happening; we shouldn't ignore the potential need to flee our homes and our cities so rapidly that we don't have time to go in the house and grab our cloaks. Or to put that in a more modern context, to go into our homes and grab our bug out bags.

It is interesting that the Lord should give this advice. Many preppers and preparedness minded people today see the priority as preparing to bug in and shelter at home when confronted by a disaster. Yet the Lord is saying the opposite. Not only is he saying to bug out, but He is saying to do so quickly. That's advice we can't afford to ignore.

DISASTERS PILING UP ON US

If there's one thing that the year 2020 has shown us, it's that disasters don't necessarily come one at a time, lined up nice and neat in a row, with time to recover in-between. They can pile up on us, overwhelming us with sheer numbers of problems to deal with whenever they want. While some of the disasters reported during this year turned out to be nothing to be concerned about, enough were significant and able to cause us problems while having to deal with other problems.

More than any other thing, the COVID-19 pandemic has defined 2020. It brought about shortages of every sort imaginable. On top of that, many people had to deal with demonstrations and rioting in their cities, while trying to protect themselves from the pandemic. Others have had to deal with hurricanes, wildfires, flooding, and tornadoes. None of these natural disasters has taken a back seat, waiting for the pandemic to pass. It was their time and they came, regardless of whether or not they were convenient for us or not.

We can expect this to continue. Regardless of what anyone says, COVID-19 isn't likely to go away. As I said earlier, the idea of a vaccine to eliminate this disease is not much of a possibility. For a vaccine to work, the antibodies that it causes our bodies to create have to be permanent; yet antibodies from COVID only last in the body for a few months. It is possible for someone to catch it again, even if their body overcame it once before.

That being the case, about the only way a vaccine would be effective would be to vaccinate pretty much the entire population at once. It would have to be worldwide, considering the amount of air travel there now is. But even that probably wouldn't be enough; it would take multiple rounds of vaccinations to keep it from spreading, mostly because we'll never get everyone to take the vaccination.

What this means is that from now on, all disasters we face will be dealt with in a COVID-19 world. Put another way, it means that every disaster we face from now on will be a situation of multiple disasters happening at the same time. That's what we need to learn to deal with.

This is different than what preppers have been planning for before. We've always worked under the assumption that there would be only one disaster at a time. While some things, like an EMP (electromagnetic pulse), would mean that a large number of things stopped working at the same time, it was still one disaster. But we can't count on that idea anymore. From now on, we must think in terms of multiple disasters, not only multiple disasters, but continuous disasters.

As mentioned earlier, 2020 has become a wry joke, with people asking "who had disaster X for Y month" every time a new disaster is on the rise. While that was intended as a joke, there have been enough things happening this year to call it the disaster of the month club.

In consequence, we need to be constantly preparing, even while in the midst of a disaster. If what we are experiencing right now is any indication of what we are heading into, in the beginning of sorrows, we are going to be seeing a constant string of disasters, without really much of a chance to recover between them.

This shouldn't be too surprising, considering all the disasters that will be happening during the Great Tribulation. If you just take the 7 seals, 7 trumpets and 7 bowls, you get 21 really major disasters. Over a three-and-a-half-year time period, that's one major worldwide disaster every two months. That may not seem like much, compared to what has happened in 2020; but remember that these are worldwide events. They're not even in the same league as two hurricanes in the Gulf of Mexico at the same time; those still qualify as regional events. Each event foretold in the Book of Revelations is going to happen around the world. We're talking about worldwide war, famine, disease, hail, fire, waters turned to blood and death.

The reality we will be facing during this time is serious from a survival point of view. We generally need a considerable amount of recovery time between disasters. Just look at how long it has taken some of our cities to recover from major hurricanes, earthquakes, or floods. It's not the kind of thing that can be done in a few short weeks. In many cases, it is the work of years. But it looks like we're not going to have those years.

Ok, so how do we prepare, while we are living through a disaster?

- Buy what you need when you see it. One of the biggest problems we face in an ongoing crisis situation is that of the stores running short of supplies. By buying things when they are available, you are able to keep your stockpile of supplies up. Always assume you need more than you do, so you don't run out.

- If you see a piece of survival equipment you might need, buy it if you can – It's easy to be penny wise and pound foolish in difficult times. While it is always nice to save money, it's more important to save your life and that of your family. If you even think you might need it, assume you will and spend the money.

- Keep your ear to the news. While it is becoming harder and harder to find any news sources we can trust, we have to try. Keeping abreast of what's happening in the world can give you an early idea of coming shortages, such as the meat shortages that happened during the early days of COVID-19, due to the slaughterhouses closing down from internal cases. Try to find reliable sources to listen to rather than opinions being passed off as news in the mainstream news media.

- Try to look ahead. None of us are issued a crystal ball that tells us what is coming, but we do have a mind and we can use it to try and figure out the future. We won't always succeed, but each success is one less thing that can catch you by surprise.

- Stay prepared. Keep your car loaded and your survival gear close at hand at all times. With so many different things happening, you never know when you will be caught by something unaware. An empty trunk in your car doesn't help you, but a trunk full of survival gear just might.

The key here is realizing that we're living in different times. While our needs and desires probably haven't changed, the world we are living in has. Because of those changes, we have to prioritize differently. So while our family might still want to go to Disney World for vacation, we have to balance that against making sure we have the necessary stockpile of supplies and equipment to ensure our survival.

SPECIFIC PROBLEMS JESUS WARNED US ABOUT

While it may not be a good idea to use the events Jesus refers to in Matthew 24 as a checklist for His return, there's a reason why he talks about the specific items he did. Since He mentions them, we should expect all of them to occur as part of the beginning of sorrows.

Knowing this, we need to make the necessary preparations for each of those items. That way, when they do happen, we will be ready. At the same time, we shouldn't limit our preparedness to only those things that Jesus mentions in this chapter, as there's always the chance that disasters will happen that He hasn't mentioned. There is no place in the chapter where he says that His list is all-inclusive.

Impersonators of Christ and False Prophets

While it might not seem important to the world, we must start with the spiritual aspect of this and not just because Jesus did. The most obvious signs of Jesus' return will be that those who are pretending to be Him, as well as false prophets pointing to a false Christ and false signs. This is a greater danger to those of us in the church than to those who are outside. While those who have never accepted Jesus Christ as their Lord and Savior will accept a false Christ, they are unsaved either way. But what of the one who has accepted Christ and falls for an imposter? How does that affect their salvation?

Don't get the idea that this is something new. There have been imposters of Christ from the early days of the church. There were false prophets even before that time. Satan is always looking for ways to lead people astray and always providing a false imitation of everything that God does for real.

Our only protection is to understand what scripture says, knowing more than just John 3:16. When we know the truth, it is much easier to discern the false. Jesus gives us very specific things to look for in His return, later in the Matthew 24, so there is no reason for any of us to be led astray, less we haven't bothered to learn what our Lord has said.

"Immediately after the tribulation of those days shall the sun be darkened, and the moon shall not give her light, and the stars shall fall from heaven, and the powers of the heavens shall be shaken [30] and then shall appear the sign of the Son of man in heaven: and then shall all the tribes of the earth mourn, and they shall see the Son of man coming in the clouds of heaven with power and great glory" (Matthew 24:29-30).

Wars

War can be a very challenging thing to survive, because the whole purpose of war is to defeat an enemy; or to put it a bit more accurately, to destroy their ability to fight back. While that may mean killing them, it can mean inflicting injury on them as well. Unfortunately, not all armies are trained to protect civilian life. Many just look at that collateral damage as a "cost of doing business."

This is especially true of terrorists, who use violence against the civilian population to try and bring about a desired political outcome. In today's world, more and more of the warfare we face is "asymmetrical warfare," propagated by terrorist organizations.

Most terrorism today is initiated by radical Muslim groups, and the vast majority of their attacks are against other Muslims. This is not to say that they make an effort to avoid attacking others. The most serious terrorist attack against our country was the downing of the twin towers on 9-11. There have been many other attacks since then, although they have not been that spectacular, and not all have been categorized as terrorist incidence.

In this sort of warfare, there is no safe place where one can go. A disgruntled worker or student attacking his or her workmates can be a terrorist incident, if the disgruntled person made contact on the dark web with one of the many websites dedicated to recruiting potential terrorists. Such incidents have happened in the past and they continue, even though the FBI is working hard to prevent them.

Our military might cannot fully protect us from this type of attack. Unlike a war in Europe, Korea or the Middle East, this form of warfare is occurring on our home turf. Worse than that, it is happening among the civilian population, not in any declared war zone. The military can't protect us, because the military isn't where the attacks are happening.

The only true protection from today's warfare is the ability to defend ourselves. Shortly after the Charlie Hebdo shooting in Paris, France, two gunmen tried a similarly motivated attack in Texas, where they were unsuccessful. In that case, two police officers took out the terrorist before they could kill any civilians. But considering that they were in Texas, the outcome probably wouldn't have been much different had the officers not been there.

There are so many people who carry a concealed weapon in Texas that the attitude amongst law enforcement is that if there is a terrorist incident in their city or town, no law enforcement officer will need to draw a gun; armed citizens will take care of it. This is our only true protection against this sort of warfare. We can't expect the government to protect us, as they will most likely be out of position when the attack comes. Terrorists aren't going to start shooting right in front of a police officer. They want to take out as many victims as possible, not be shot by the police before they accomplish anything, like the two in Dallas.

Besides being able to shoot back, we should seriously consider building our family a shelter where they will be safe from attack, either a safe room or bunker. Should war reach our communities, this could be a way of protecting them, without having to fight in the war. If we are forced to fight, there's always the possibility that we will die.

If we are not prepared to protect ourselves and our families, we are not prepared for this or any other kind of war. While it would be better to avoid war altogether, that may not always be possible. When it is not, it is critical that we have the necessary firearms to protect ourselves and also the knowledge of how to use them effectively, including the necessary infantry tactics that will allow us to fight, without exposing ourselves unnecessarily.

Famines

The history of the world has been plagued with times of famine. We even see it referenced in the Book of Genesis, as the reason why Joseph and his sons went down to Egypt. But Jesus mentioning it here makes it seem like he's talking about worldwide famine, not just a local event.

There are several ways that a worldwide famine would be possible. Probably the most drastic of these would be if the Yellowstone Supervolcano erupted. In that case, the ash from the volcano would cover most of the Midwest, the "Great American Breadbasket", where most of our grain is grown. But that's not all it would do; it would send a cloud of ash into the upper atmosphere, where it would encircle the Earth, cutting down the amount of sunlight reaching the planet.

Something like that happened in 1816, known as "the year without a summer." In that case, it was Mount Tambora in Indonesia that erupted in the largest volcanic eruption in recorded history. But due to the size of the Yellowstone Caldera, that eruption would be nothing. Summer temperatures in the year without a summer were the coldest on record, causing food shortages across the Northern Hemisphere.

In the case of a potential Yellowstone eruption, the amount of ash that would be pushed into the upper atmosphere would be so great that it might cause more than one such year, leading to food shortages worldwide. Without the major food producing and exporting nations providing food to countries that don't produce enough, starvation would kill off millions.

Of course, it's widely believed that an EMP attack would cause a famine as well, although that would be limited to the countries attacked by the EMP. Even so, the idea of an EMP, followed by misunderstanding and retaliation, could result in much of the world living without electricity and ending up in famine.

Regardless of the cause of the famine, the only way to

make sure that it doesn't affect you and me is to make sure that we are self-sufficient and able to grow our own food. That way, even if there is a worldwide famine, we can grow our own food, keeping our family fed, even in the midst of a famine.

This may actually be harder than it seems, considering that the famine could be caused by something that would make it hard to grow crops. If there isn't enough light or water, then growing at home isn't going to be any easier than growing on a farm. About the only way around this would be with artificial light. That's possible, but it would require a lot of electricity. It would need to be a situation where there was still electricity, even though there was a problem with sunlight or water.

In either case, being ready to grow your own food, as well as having a good stockpile of food on hand is the only way you can protect yourself from famine. How big a stockpile and how long it will last is the real question.

Pestilences

By definition, COVID-19 is a pestilence, so we're already seeing what pestilence can do to the world. It has shut down commerce across the globe, causing massive economic hardship for tens or even hundreds of millions of people. While COVID has not had as high a death toll as some epidemics in the past, it has been bad enough to get the world's attention.

Keep in mind that this is the first worldwide pandemic

ever other than HIV/AIDS and a few variants of the flu. While there have been other pandemics, they have not been worldwide like this one. Even the Black Death, which devastated Europe, didn't go beyond those borders to other continents.

Looking at the damage that the current pandemic has done to the world, and especially to the world's economy, it is clear that pestilence has a massive amount of destructive power, even in today's highly technical world. It is possibly even more destructive than any time in the past.

We first heard about the novel coronavirus on December 31st of 2019. It wasn't but two weeks later that the U.S. had its first case. By the beginning of March, things had become serious and our state and local governments were looking at measures to slow the spread, specifically using lockdowns. At the same time, Italy was at its peak, with thousands of new cases recorded per day. The mayor of the Italian city that was the epicenter warned us that we would be seeing the same thing in two weeks, and he was right.

The problem today is that any such disease can spread faster than our medical community can study it. That's where the real danger comes in. Air travel makes it easy for disease to spread, especially with the massive amount of international air travel for business. This makes it possible for any disease to become a worldwide pandemic within weeks, just like COVID-19 did.

Fortunately, there are things we can do to protect

ourselves from any disease. More than anything, avoiding contact with others and isolating ourselves from others will help keep us disease-free, even in the midst of a pandemic. We see it happening during the COVID-19 pandemic, and we can expect the same safety measures to help us in any future pandemic.

The big thing here is to have enough personal protection equipment (PPE) and disinfectants on hand. The shortages we've seen from COVID-19 will most likely repeat themselves with any future pandemic. So, we have to be ready. Of course, in any really serious pandemic that is more contagious and deadly than COVID-19, just having PPE isn't going to be enough. In that case, we're probably going to need to isolate ourselves, even away from our population centers. That's pretty much what people did to survive the Black Plague. If it worked for them, it will work for us as well.

Earthquakes

Earthquakes have long been a concern, especially in earthquake-prone areas of the world, like the "Ring of Fire" around the Pacific Ocean. One of the most dangerous natural disasters there is, earthquakes can't be predicted, and they can't be avoided, unless it is by living far away from the areas where earthquakes happen.

As far as danger is concerned, earthquakes are only superseded by major floods for total death count, although the top eleven deadliest natural disasters are all earthquakes. Hurricanes cause more total damage as measured in dollars, but that's mostly because of flooding damaging or the destruction of a huge number of buildings over a larger area. Earthquakes don't just cause flood damage; they can totally destroy buildings.

From a purely human viewpoint, earthquakes are terrifying. The suddenness of them coming on, along with the total lack of warning, catches people by surprise, without the ability to prepare themselves mentally and emotionally for what is about to come. Earthquakes also have the ability to cause other disasters, such as tsunamis. The Fukashima Daiichi nuclear power plant disaster in northeastern Japan was caused by a tsunami, which was in turn caused by an earthquake. While the reactors automatically shut down fission reaction when the earthquake was detected, that didn't stop the damage caused by the tsunami flooding the plant's generators, preventing the necessary safety measures from kicking in.

This is a perfect example of what multiple simultaneous disasters can do. The Fukashima Daiichi nuclear power plant was probably designed with earthquakes in mind, as Japan has always suffered from a lot of them. Had they just had an earthquake, even as strong an earthquake as happened on that fateful day, the power plant's automatic safety shutdown procedure would have prevented the problems with meltdowns and radiation leaks that happened. But when the tsunami came, that second disaster prevented all those safety measures from taking place.

According to the World Nuclear Association, 20% of

the world's nuclear reactors are operating in earthquake danger zones. While nuclear power plants are designed for this, with failsafe procedures in place to protect the power plant in the event of an emergency, the Fukashima Daiichi disaster proves that those measures probably aren't sufficient.

Should earthquakes ever occur on a worldwide basis, there is no telling how much damage they could cause. Up until now, earthquakes have been localized events. But with so many of the world's geological fault lines circling the Pacific Ocean, could there ever be a cascading effect? If so, how severe might the damage be?

As I mentioned earlier, there is almost nothing we can do to prepare or protect ourselves from an earthquake, except to be somewhere else. Moving is an option I would seriously consider if I lived in an earthquake zone.

Persecution of Christians

Christians are currently persecuted in fifty of the world's 195 countries. I'm not talking about the "they talked bad about us" type of persecution either. I'm talking about the kind where Christians are beaten or killed. That's happening today in many places, without us even seeing it. As for the rest of the world, hatred of Christianity is one of the few "socially acceptable" forms of prejudice there is. Nobody gets called out by the media, the "social justice police" or the "woke left" for hating Christians. On the contrary, Christians are more likely to be called out by those groups, even if they have to invent something to call

Christians out for.

With the socialist push going on in much of the world, especially Western Europe and the United States, it seems likely that Christian persecution will increase. Socialism and communism are jealous gods and don't allow Christianity to exist in the open. Then there's Islam, the world's fastest growing religion. As Muslims take over countries, they push for Sharia Law, which makes apostasy a crime. Many of those fifty countries where Christians are currently persecuted are controlled by Muslims. The more countries they control, the more persecution there will be. Islam, even more than communism, does not allow competing religions to exist.

This is a spiritual battle and should be treated as one. But more than that, we need to prepare ourselves for the coming persecution. Jesus gave us this warning not so we could escape from it, but so that we could be ready for it. We will need to be strong in faith to carry us through.

Iniquity Abounding

This is something else we see going on around us, each and every day. We are living in times where good is being called bad and bad is being called good. The mainstream media that controls what most people hear about the world around them has become a political machine, fully in bed with one political party. While I won't say that the opposing party is perfect, the party the media is connected with is taking a stance on many issues that goes clearly against God's Word.

The idea of killing unborn babies for convenience sake is totally against the teachings of the Bible. In contrast, the early church rescued Roman babies who were left to die as an offering to the gods. Violence, rioting, and looting are being allowed in many places, not just in the United States, but in many parts of Europe and around the world. Whether the rioters are Muslim "refugees" or anarchists is immaterial. The fact that governments are allowing this sort of lawlessness, without consequence, is perhaps without precedent and shows just how fragile a condition society is in.

Just as George Orwell wrote in "1984," good is called evil and evil is called good. Those who do iniquity are not even being chastised for it, even when they are destroying the lives of others. At the same time, those who call them out are finding themselves condemned in the court of public opinion.

I remember a time when Hollywood was driving people more and more towards iniquity, but not today. The loudest voices condemning good and promoting evil are found on social media today. The mob mentality of social media is making demands of society, which their numbers do not justify. But because their voice is so loud, they make themselves seem to be the majority, drowning out any other voice.

Our biggest concern is not to allow ourselves to be caught up in it. We are still supposed to be a light to this world (Matt 5:14), and the darker the world becomes, the brighter we should shine. To do so, we must keep ourselves away from politics, arguments on social media, and allowing ourselves to be sucked into the outrage that is fueling the mob. Even for things we agree with, if they are not what the Bible says, we best keep silent.

Love of Many Waxing Cold

Finally, Jesus talked about love, or more correctly, the lack of love. As people become more and more self-focused, seeking something to make themselves feel good about themselves, they lose the ability to see others as anything but a tool to get what they need. Rather than reaching out in love to those around them, they reach out to suck the love out of others, without giving anything in return.

Granted, we are all born selfish; that's part of the human condition. But the difference we're seeing today is that it is becoming normalized. Just a few short years ago, those in the world defined morality as not doing anything that would hurt another. That definition is being changed today. It only matters whether your words and actions hurt certain types and classes of people. It's considered okay to hurt others, especially if you do so in an effort to help those who are supposed to be protected.

This sort of confusion is only going to increase. There is literally nothing that can be done to stop it. Even so, it serves a purpose. It creates a backdrop to show the love of Jesus Christ to this world - a backdrop that will make His love shine all the brighter.

Jesus left us with one "new commandment" to fulfill. If ever there was a time when the world needed that commandment, it is now.

"A new commandment I give unto you, that you love one another; even as I have loved you, that you also love one another" (John 13:34).

We can say that it is important that the love of many grows cold, just as we can say that it is important that iniquity abounds. What makes it important is that when used properly, it provides us with an excellent opportunity to show Christ's character to this hurt and dying world. The more that the world accepts these things, the more we can show Jesus. That's our job during this time that He refers to as the "beginning of sorrows." Perhaps in all that sorrow, we can be the ones to bring a little comfort.

LIVING THE GREAT ESCAPE

Jesus gives some very clear direction as to what we should do in this time He calls the beginning of sorrows. Of course, that means knowing exactly what time He is referring to. He said:

"When ye therefore shall see the abomination of desolation, spoken of by Daniel the prophet, stand in the holy place, (whoso readeth, let him understand)" (Matthew 24:15).

As mentioned earlier, many theologians and commentators talk about this verse as referring to the Roman army, thought to be an abomination due to their pagan religious beliefs and known in that time for the destruction they brought. However, those same commentators talk about this chapter in reference to the End Times. So which is it? Is it talking about something that happened 2,000 years ago or something yet to come? It's quite possible that it speaks of both. Jesus is clearly talking about events yet to come here, at least from His perspective. That makes His statement clearly prophetic. In many cases, prophecy has a dual meaning, one that happened in the near-term for those who heard the prophecy and a long-term meaning that applies to the End Times. This could be what we're seeing here.

In this case, the advice that Jesus is giving can be applied to the events that He refers to earlier in the chapter, specifically those referred to as signs of the end of the age. With that understanding, it is clear that Jesus' advice to those who read and understand is to flee the city. He says:

"Then let them which be in Judea flee into the mountains; [17] Let him which is on the housetop not come down to take anything out of his house: [18] Neither let him which is in the field return back to take his clothes… [20] But pray ye that your flight be not in the winter, neither on the Sabbath day" (Matthew 24:16-20).

Why does Jesus say to flee to the mountains? This isn't a casual statement, nor is it the kind of fear mongering we see people engaging in today. Remember, He was talking to His closest disciples here, not just anyone. So if He wants them to flee, He has good reason for giving them the advice.

I must say, this goes clearly against the common wisdom in the prepping movement today. Most survival writers will recommend sheltering in your home, rather than bugging out. Not only that, but they won't recommend bugging out to the wilderness. If you have to bug out, they'll say either go to a prepared survival shelter or to some rural town where you can find shelter.

Nevertheless, this is the Lord talking, so I'm sure that He's right and everyone else is wrong. But why is He giving this advice? Perhaps we can get a hint if we look at the types of disasters He mentions in the beginning of the chapter.

- Wars and rumors of wars (vs. 6) – Wars can happen anywhere, and for the last couple of hundred years they have largely been fought in wide open spaces. But this has changed recently, with most wars happening in urban areas. Urban warfare is much more dangerous to civilians, especially when terrorist groups are involved. They will use civilians as human shields, sacrificing the lives of those civilians to protect their own. The only way to avoid this is to avoid being in the cities where such warfare is happening.

- Famines (vs. 7) – When famine comes, those who are hit the hardest are the people living in the cities. While there may not be much food available anywhere, the competition for food is always fiercest in the city, due to the higher number of people seeking the same resources. Rural areas might not have much more, but there are fewer people competing for those resources that do exist. Rural farming communities may even have more resources available.

- Pestilences (vs. 7) – As we've recently seen with COVID-19, places with higher population concentrations are prime areas for the spread of disease. While plenty of smaller cities have had serious outbreaks of the coronavirus, the majority of the cases have been in big cities. Some smaller communities have managed to remain untouched.

- Earthquakes (vs. 7) – It doesn't matter where you are, earthquakes are devastating. But if you're in the city, especially the city center with all the tall buildings, then the chances of being crushed under falling debris are greater. You can still get hurt by an earthquake out in the wild, but your chances of surviving it are greater, as long as there isn't an avalanche.

- Believers delivered up to death (vs. 8) – Persecution of believers is much more likely to happen in population centers than in the wilderness. Those who persecute want to make an example of the people they are persecuting, especially if they are killing them. The more people who can see what is happening, the better for them.

- Many will be offended (vs. 10) – We see this happening today. But where is it happening? In the big cities. This doesn't seem to be happening in rural America.

- False prophets deceiving many (vs. 11) – Any false prophet wants an audience. So they're going to go to the biggest, most important city they can find, where they can gather a huge audience. They're definitely not going to follow Jesus' example and go out into the countryside to preach on a hillside.

- Lawlessness will abound (vs. 12) – While lawlessness can happen anywhere, the criminal element is more likely to stick to the city, where there are plenty of people to victimize. Again, we are seeing this happen in recent times with all the riots, vandalism and looting that has been happening by those who have hijacked the Black Lives Matter movement. The mob is trying to control America, and they are using lawlessness to do so. But mostly in the cities.

Looking at these items, we see one common thread; it is more dangerous to be in the city when those things are happening than to be out in the country or the wilderness. Staying in the city could very well be signing one's own death warrant, while getting out of town could save our lives. Since Jesus said to flee to the mountains, it appears that this will be the safest place in those days. Why? Perhaps because there will be less people, especially less of those likely to be killing believers. There will also be less likelihood of all the other disasters that he brought to our attention in those prophetic verses.

Just how Can We do That?

Bugging out to the mountains isn't something that should be done on a whim, without preparation. Granted, if

Jesus appeared to you and said, "go now", I'd suggest going now, whether or not you're prepared. But Jesus isn't doing that. He's giving us good warning, with plenty of time to prepare. It seems to me that it would behoove us to prepare ourselves to do just what He has told us to do.

More than anything, it means having someplace to go if you've got to get out of town and stocking the place with the equipment and supplies you'll need. But that's much easier said than done. Few of us can afford to buy a cabin in the woods. Even so, we either need such a retreat or something similar. Here are a few ideas to consider:

- If you have a family member or close friend who lives in the country, you might be able to work out an arrangement to turn their home or land into a survival retreat, teaming together for both of your benefit. As part of the arrangement, you might be able to park a travel trailer on their property for your family to stay in.

- The federal government owns a lot of uninhabited land held in public trust, especially in the western half of the country. While the use of that land is regulated, it might not be possible for the government to enforce regulations during a time of crisis. Besides, the farther you can get from inhabited areas, the less likelihood there is of patrolling by government agents.

- There is such a thing as "junk land" you can buy for less than $1,000 per acre. This is land that is unusable for any commercial or agricultural purpose, and it isn't in a good area for homes. The trick is finding it. You'll have to put out feelers and tolerate real estate agents calling you, trying to sell you something you don't want.

- Find a rural town you can go to. While any disasters that are happening are unlikely to totally miss a rural town, the lower population density will make them easier to deal with.

Finding an uninhabited area you can use might not be easy, as you really want an area that's not readily accessible. But if you enjoy backpacking, you probably know some such areas already. For that matter, if you go camping, you probably know some areas that aren't anywhere near as remote but still qualify as "flee to the mountains", as Jesus said.

A few things to keep in mind when looking for a place you can use as a retreat:

- You're going to need water. That doesn't necessarily mean you have to buy a piece of land with water on it; but water needs to be close enough that you can bring it back to your retreat.

- You're going to need wood for fuel. Since green wood produces smoke, you're better off finding a place with a lot of deadfall wood on the ground, that will give you dry wood for your fire, rather than having to cut green wood and then waiting for it to dry.

- Since you're going to be away from the city and your home, protection from the weather is important. Avoid areas that can flood and try to find a place where the contours of the land or the existing trees will protect you from the wind.

- Accessibility is important, as you're going to have to bring in everything. That may mean carting by hand. Is the location somewhere that you can practically do that?

- What food resources are available? Is there somewhere you can fish? What about hunting? Are there plants growing in the area that can be eaten for food?

- Be sure that you will be well hidden from casual view and that your camp won't attract attention. Remember, there will be persecution of believers going on during that time.

- Think about how defensible the place is. Whether or not you choose to defend yourself if you come under attack is your decision. But either way, you want to be sure that you and your family aren't sitting ducks.

- Be sure you have a good escape route, should you need to leave.

- Be sure to find a PrepperNet Group. PrepperNet is an organization of like-minded individuals who believe in personal responsibility, individual freedoms, and preparing for disasters of all origins. Being a part of a group like this is your most important prep. It's hard to survive on your own.

Regardless of where you end up finding your survival retreat, it would be a good idea to do some preparation so you have something to go to besides empty ground. While you probably can't get away with building a cabin on government land, you can find somewhere relatively close to that land to build a cache of food, survival equipment and other supplies. That way, when you flee to the mountains, you won't be without anything in order to survive.

One of the easiest ways of building a supply cache is to rent storage in some nearby town. Few towns today don't have one of those "U Store It" places, by some name or other. A small unit isn't all that expensive and can provide room for a lot of equipment and supplies. If you are able to make some connection with the people of that town, it could help you if you need to flee.

Building that Supply Cache

One of the "big concerns" about the Tribulation is the Mark of the Beast. According to the Book of Revelations:

"He (the beast) causes all, both small and great, rich and poor, free and slave, to receive a mark on their right hand or on their foreheads, [17] and that no one may buy or sell except one who has the mark of the name of the beast, or the number of his name" (Revelations 13:16-17).

While our focus in this book is the time referred to as the beginning of sorrows and not the Tribulation, the availability to purchase while in hiding is something that can't be ignored. One of the results of the COVID-19 pandemic has been a coin shortage, resulting in retail companies asking their patrons to pay with a credit or debit card, rather than cash. Some have gone so far as to stop accepting cash as a form of payment. This could provide an opportunity to those who have been pushing for a cashless society.

It is impossible to use a credit or debit card, without the bank or credit card company knowing exactly who you are. So if it becomes impossible to buy with cash, believers trying to escape persecution could be left without any option whatsoever, even if they do have money in the bank. The solution to that problem is nothing new; it is to stockpile the necessary supplies beforehand. Many have talked about that as a means of surviving the Tribulation, even among those who believe in a pre-tribulation rapture; but it doesn't seem like anyone talks about doing so to get through the beginning of sorrows.

The one big question we don't have an answer to is this, how long will the beginning of sorrows last? It seems to be something that God hasn't told us, even though He has provided some fairly good information about a timeline for the Tribulation itself.

Since there is no definitive answer, the only realistic way to proceed is to build as big a stockpile as you can. In other words, start building the stockpile and just keep adding to it, without a specific goal in mind. Whatever you manage to put in that stockpile will put you in a better situation than you are in today, with a greater chance of surviving difficult times.

So, what needs to be in this supply stockpile? Here are some basics:

- o Food – You'll want to have non-perishable food packaged for long-term storage. This includes:

  - o Beans
  - o Rice
  - o Canned food
  - o Dried food
  - o Grains for baking
  - o Baking supplies (baking powder, baking soda, etc.)
  - o Dried milk and eggs
  - o Salt, spices and bouillon (soup stock)
  - o Pasta
  - o Nuts & nut butters
  - o Coffee & tea
  - o Sauces
  - o Cooking oil

- • Water – Hopefully your survival retreat will be close to a supply of water. Even so, it's a good idea to have some in your cache.

- Means to purify water – Most of your water will need to come from nature, but you'll have to purify it, assuming that it isn't safe to drink.

- Fire starters and fuel – To keep you warm and cook your food. Granted, you can probably gather wood from the forest floor, but an alternative fuel source for emergencies is a good idea

- Batteries – To power flashlights and small electronics

- Backup power – To charge batteries and small electronics, including smart phones (be sure to turn off the tracking feature)

- First-aid supplies – In case of injury. You may not be able to go to a doctor

- Medicines – Stock over-the-counter medicines, antibiotics, and any prescription medicines needed for treating chronic conditions that family members suffer from

- Ammunition – Both to defend yourself with and to hunt

- Personal hygiene supplies – Cleanliness is important in maintaining your health

- Cleaning supplies – For the same reason

- Survival tools – The necessary tools to harvest what you need from nature and to build a shelter

Granted, this list is by no means complete; it contains merely the most important items. In reality, you will need anything that anyone else needs for a long-term survival situation. Even so, much will depend on your personal situation and your survival retreat.

Before building too big a cache, you need to have a place to keep it. If you are able to come up with some sort of permanent survival retreat, like a cabin in the woods or a travel trailer on a family member's property in the country, you'll be establishing your supply cache there as well. But if you don't have such a place, you'll need to find someplace you can build the cache, such as a rental storage locker in a rural town close to the area you intend to bug out to.

In either case, you may find yourself limited by storage space, making it difficult to build a large supply cache. In the case of building the cache in a rental storage space, you will somehow have to move everything to your survival retreat. That may mean moving it on foot, if your survival retreat is far enough into the boonies that you can't drive there.

THE MOST IMPORTANT PREPARATION

While physically preparing for the beginning of sorrows is important, it is nowhere near as important as spiritually preparing for it. Regardless of what physical challenges we face, we need to depend on the Lord. That means having a relationship with Him, so that we can call upon Him for help.

I'm not just referring to getting saved and having eternalsalvation. Yes, that's important; but going through the motions of saying the prayer of salvation isn't the same as having a relationship with Jesus. It's merely the first step in the process. If we expect His help in times of trouble, then we need to know how to talk to Him. It needs to become a habit. We need to know what He has promised to do, so that we ask in accordance with His will. After all, He won't do otherwise. More than anything, we need to develop the habit of going to Him first with our needs, rather than as a last resort.

There is no promise written into the Bible that says that God will keep us from problems and difficulties, as some people seem to think. Rather, God says that He will see us through those times, protecting us in the midst of the storm, rather than protecting us from the storm.

"When you pass through the waters, I will be with you; and through the rivers, they shall not overflow you. When you walk through the fire, you shall not be burned, nor shall the flame scorch you" (Isaiah 43:2)

Note that this verse doesn't say that when we pass through the waters, God will build us a bridge. Nor does it say that when we walk though fire, he will quench the flames. The only thing it says is that the water and flames won't hurt us and not that we will get out of them.

Remember the poem "Footprints in the Sand?" It's not scripture, but it is beautiful, nevertheless. That poem is the story of a man who had a dream about footprints on a beach, which represented the course of his life. Most of the time, there were two sets of footprints - his own and the Lord's. But he noticed that during some of the darkest hours of his life, there was only one set. Asking the Lord about this, he received the answer that during those times, the Lord had carried him.

That's how the Lord is when we are His. He doesn't discriminate amongst us, but offers the same to all. Even so, that doesn't mean that He carries all of us through every possible situation. While He offers that to all, not all accept what He has to offer. Just like salvation, we need to be willing to receive every gift He intends to give us.

This is where the problem lies. If we are going to make it through this time, it isn't enough to say a prayer of salvation. We need to learn how to depend on Him. We need to get to the point where we are accustomed to looking to Him for our needs, especially in times of crisis, rather than looking to what we can do ourselves.

Just as there are many who turn their back on Jesus' offer of salvation, there are many who call themselves by His name, yet still turn away from His help, perhaps unintentionally. It's not that they don't want His help, but rather that they aren't ready to receive it when it comes.

This is why it is so important that we develop the faith of a child. Children don't just have faith sometimes; they have faith all the time. It never stops. There isn't that moment when they say, "Maybe I shouldn't jump, because daddy might not catch me." No, they jump, with full security in their hearts that daddy will be there and he will catch them.

Likewise, Jesus will be there to catch us. It doesn't matter what happens during those times of tribulation, He will be there for us. He will help us to pass through the water without drowning and walk through the fire without burning.

Does this mean that we shouldn't prepare? No, I don't believe so; there are many times in scripture where God tells people to prepare. He's the one who invented the idea of prepping, as well as the idea of bugging out. His first student in this was Noah, who God instructed to build the world's largest floating zoo, even though Noah didn't have a single animal to fill it. Yet, when the time came, God brought the animals to him.

So why didn't God just give Noah the ark? Scripture doesn't say. But there are times when God tells us to do something as a test of our faith. Building that ark could have been Noah's test. By obeying and doing what God had directed him to do, he prepared himself for the next step, going in and allowing God to close the door and shut him in.

Had Noah not had to go through the experience of building the ark, trusting God for all those years, how well would he have done when it was time for the rain to start? Would he have taken his family into the ark? Would he have accepted all those animals? Would he have had the faith he needed so that he could trust God to take care of him and his family? I doubt it.

Your preparation for the beginning of sorrows can be seen as your test, preparing you for the time when God will take you out of society and up to the mountains so you will miss out on the disasters that will happen. Remember, Jesus said that when we see those signs, we are to flee. He didn't say that the heavens would part, a light would descend over us, and a deep voice with lots of reverb would tell us it was time to "get hither unto our abode of safety." No, when that time comes, we will have to recognize it and move by faith.

This is the great challenge - moving by faith. Not faith in ourselves or what we have done, but faith in Him, knowing that He has our best interests at heart. Those who have learned how to follow Him, walking in faith, will be the ones who flee to the hills, as He has instructed. The others, who have hemmed and hawed about getting ready, will continue to hem and haw while they are overtaken by those problems.

Which will you be?

ABOUT THE AUTHOR

F orrest Garvin is a former US Air Force NCO who served with the 317 MAC and JSOC SOLLII out of Pope Air Force Base. After leaving the military, Garvin worked in the technology field for the Strategic Technology Group for NationsBank/Bank of America and then went on to create several technology startups. Garvin is a survival instructor, NRA instructor, general license HAM operator, Krav Maga apprentice instructor, speaker, educator, radio/podcast host, and author. Garvin has been a prepper since Y2K. Garvin also owns the Carolina Survival & Preparedness Academy in Charlotte, NC. His survival academy offers courses in self-defense, homesteading, firearms, family preparedness and survival skills. In addition, he consults with preppers and survival groups around the USA. Garvin was the founder of the Carolina Preppers Network, which now is PrepperNet. PrepperNet has over 54,500 members nationwide.

RESOURCES

Stand Firm to the End Website:

http://forrestgarvin.com

Authors Website:

http://forrestgarvin.com

Preppers Consulting:

https://preppersconsulting.com

Link to online resources:

https://forrestgarvin.com/resources

Want to know more about the Christian Faith?

Billy Graham Evangelistic Association:

https://peacewithgod.net

PrepperNet is the place to meet, network & find other preppers, homesteaders & survivalist.

If you are not in a group… You will die.

For more resources and tools join us at PrepperNet's Website: https://preppernet.com

Signup for our Newsletter

Get a Free Bug Out Bag Check List

The Prepping Academy Radio Show!

Prepping Academy Radio Show is a live broadcast where we discuss all things prepping, survival and self-reliance. Our Goal at The Prepping Academy Radio Show is to expand your thinking & motivate you to take action – because it's time that we get prepared.

Host: Forrest, Kyle & Tenderfoot

Website: https://preppingacademy.com

GOD BLESS!